Beetles

This book has been reviewed
for accuracy by
Walter L. Gojmerac
Professor of Entomology
University of Wisconsin—Madison.

Library of Congress Cataloging in Publication Data

Oda, Hidetomo.
 Beetles.

 (Nature close-ups)
 Translation of: Kabutomushi / text by Hidetomo Oda,
photographs by Hidekazu Kubo.
 Summary: Discusses the life cycle, behavior patterns,
and habitats of beetles.
 1. Beetles—Juvenile literature. [1. Beetles]
I. Kubo, Hidekazu, ill. II. Title. III. Series.
QL576.2.03313 1986   595.76'4   85-28235

ISBN 0-8172-2530-7 (lib. bdg.)
ISBN 0-8172-2555-2 (softcover)

This edition first published in 1986 by Raintree Publishers Inc.

Text copyright © 1986 by Raintree Publishers Inc., translated by Jun
Amano from *Beetles* copyright © 1977 by Jun Nanao and Hidetomo
Oda.

Photographs copyright © 1977 by Hidekazu Kubo.

World English translation rights for *Color Photo Books on Nature*
arranged with Kaisei-Sha through Japan Foreign-Rights Center.

1 2 3 4 5 6 7 8 9 0   90 89 88 87 86

Beetles

Raintree Publishers
Milwaukee

◀ **Children looking for beetles.**

Some beetles live underground, others live on plant leaves and stems, or in the bark of trees. Beetles are hearty eaters, although their diets vary from species to species. Generally, beetles can be found close to their favorite food source.

Acorns

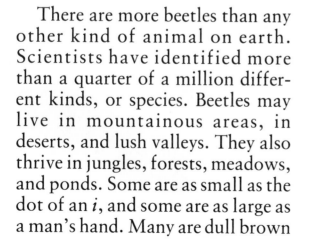

There are more beetles than any other kind of animal on earth. Scientists have identified more than a quarter of a million different kinds, or species. Beetles may live in mountainous areas, in deserts, and lush valleys. They also thrive in jungles, forests, meadows, and ponds. Some are as small as the dot of an *i*, and some are as large as a man's hand. Many are dull brown or black. Others are green, gold, or blue and shine with a jewel-like brilliance. The tiny red ladybug, the fat June bug, and the flickering firefly are all kinds of beetles. The ferocious-looking rhinoceros beetle in this book is just one of the many kinds of beetles which scientists group in the scarab beetle family.

▼ **Beetles feeding on tree sap.** In summer, trees have plenty of sap. In this photo, a rhinoceros beetle (upper) and stag beetles (lower) feed on the sap of an oak tree.

▼ Pupae in their underground pupal chambers.

The male pupa (left) has horns, but the female (right) does not. Male rhinoceros beetles are known for their horns. However, many beetles have no horns at all.

► The pupa develops.

The pupa is light-colored at first, but eventually it darkens. Gradually, the adult beetle's body becomes visible through the protective skin. The legs, wings, antennae, mouth, and eyes of the adult beetle are being formed.

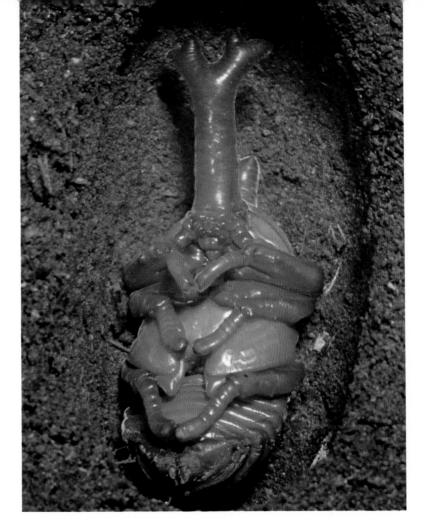

Although beetles may look very different from one another, their body structure and development are similar. Beetles go through four definite stages of growth, called complete metamorphosis. All beetles begin life as eggs, the first stage in their life cycle. When the eggs hatch, larvae emerge. The larvae are caterpillar-like creatures that do not look anything like adult beetles. Larvae have huge appetites and spend most of their time eating and growing. When they have grown big enough, they are ready to enter the third stage of their life cycle, as pupae.

When the beetle larva is ready to pupate, it burrows a hole in the ground or inside tree bark, depending on the species of beetle. It lies still inside its pupal chamber and lives on stored food as its body begins to form into an adult.

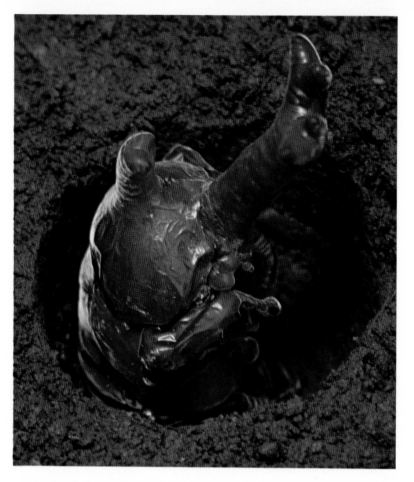

◄ A beetle begins to emerge.

When the adult's body is fully formed inside the pupal skin, the body turns dark, except for the wings and abdomen. The strong spines on the legs begin to rip through the protective skin.

► The head and thorax appear.

When the horns break through the skin, the head and midsection, thorax, appear. They are already hard and black. The adult beetle's eyes and mouth are located at the base of the horns.

The pupa is light-colored at first, but darkens as its protective skin forms and hardens. In time, the outline of the adult beetle's body becomes visible through the pupal skin. It takes about a month for the adult rhinoceros beetle to fully develop during this resting stage. Some kinds of beetles rest through the entire winter as pupae.

By moving and stretching its legs and horns, the beetle cracks the hard pupal skin and slowly emerges. First, the spiny, hardened front and middle legs break through the skin. But the back legs do not move yet because they are close to the fragile wings and could easily damage them.

▶ Legs breaking through the skin.

Every time the beetle stretches and moves its legs, the protective pupal skin tears. First, the spiny front and middle legs emerge. Then the beetle carefully sheds the rest of its skin, so as not to damage the fragile wings and soft abdomen.

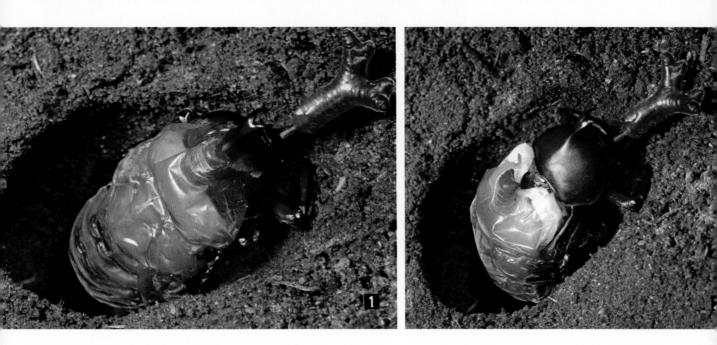

● **The beetle emerges (photos 1-4).** Using the first two pairs of legs, the beetle pushes off the rest of its pupal skin and wriggles out. The skin covering the tips of the horns comes off when the beetle crawls out of the ground.

As its horns break through the front of the pupal skin, the beetle's head appears. It is already hardened and dark in color. Using its front and middle legs, the beetle carefully removes the remaining pupal skin, pushing it down little by little. Finally, the soft, pale wings and abdomen, the rear part of its body, come out. Both pairs of wings are stretched out to dry. Within twenty-four hours, the wings harden. At the same time, the abdomen, as well as the wings, darkens, and the beetle's metamorphosis is complete. Only then will the rhinoceros beetle leave the pupal chamber to begin its life as an adult.

▶ **The beetle stretches its wings (photo 5).**

After shedding its pupal skin, the beetle stretches out its thin hind wings to dry. After drying, the beetle uses its hind legs to fold the back wings under the hard, front wings.

◀ **The front wings take on color and harden.**

Adult beetles eat a variety of things, depending on the species. They have mouth parts called mandibles, which are jaws that move from side to side like scissors. Some beetles are herbivorous. They eat plants, tree leaves and bark, and crops. Others are predators and hunt insects and other small animal prey. Some are scavengers. They eat dead animals and insects. These rhinoceros beetles are feeding on the sweet juices of fruits and the sap of oak trees.

◄ **An adult rhinoceros beetle.**

Once the beetle leaves its pupal chamber, it begins life above ground, as an adult.

▲ **Beetles feeding on tree sap.** Rhinoceros beetles and stag beetles gather on this tree to eat sap. Because adult beetles emerge fully grown from the pupal chamber, they eat to gain energy, not to grow.

▲ **A long-horned beetle.**

Many species of long-horned beetle larvae live in the trunks of trees. When they become adults, they cut holes in the tree bark and come out. Sap oozes from such cuts in tree bark.

▲ **A wasp biting a tree.**

Various insects will gather around a cut in tree bark to feed on the sap. Some insects, like this wasp, widen the cut by biting at the bark.

Most beetles do not have good eyesight. However, most beetles have feelers, or antennae. Beetles use their antennae to help them feel their way along and to detect food from a distance. When they sense the sweet scent of sap, the beetles use their sharp jaws to cut through the tree bark. The rhinoceros beetle's mouth is lined with whisker-like hairs which brush the sap, tasting and ingesting it. Often, other insects also gather alongside the beetles to feed on the tree sap.

◄ **A butterfly sipping tree sap.**

Some species of butterflies use their long, straw-like proboscises for sipping tree sap.

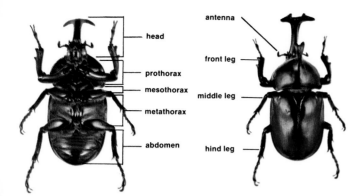

head
prothorax
mesothorax
metathorax
abdomen

antenna
front leg
middle leg
hind leg

● Body structure of a beetle.

Regardless of the species, all beetles have the same basic body structure: (1) a head with eyes, antennae, and mouth parts (close-up below), (2) a thorax with three pairs of legs and two pairs of wings, and (3) an abdomen, the rear part of the body which contains the reproductive organs.

◀ **Children searching for beetles.**

Various kinds of beetles can be found on trees and in groves such as this one.

▼ **A beetle in flight.**

The front wings, the protective elytra, are raised in flight. The thin, transparent hind wings beat the air rapidly, propelling the beetle forward.

Rhinoceros beetles are nocturnal insects. That means they are most active at night. They dislike strong sunlight. They rest under fallen leaves or at the roots of trees during the day. After sunset, they begin to fly about, searching for food.

Many beetles, especially the larger species, are clumsy fliers. Indeed, some species of ground beetles cannot fly at all, even though they have wings. The beetle's front wings form the elytra, a shell-like case which protects the thin, transparent hind wings. In flight, the elytra are raised, but they remain still. They act as a kind of glider to give the beetle "lift." The hind wings rapidly beat up and down, propelling the insect forward.

▶ **Rhinoceros beetles looking for tree sap.**

Beetles on a tree trunk at dusk, searching for tree sap.

● **Two males fighting.** The males fix themselves firmly on the tree bark, using their spiny claws, and then attack one another. Sometimes a horn is broken off or a wing is pierced in battle. Often one beetle is flipped over and falls from the tree.

With their heavily armored bodies and fierce horns, the large rhinoceros beetles are among the most ferocious-looking of all the beetles. Only the males have horns. They use them to strip bark from trees. But they also use them to protect their territory by fighting off other males.

Although many of the more than twenty thousand scarab species have horns, they are very prominent in the hercules, elephant, and rhinoceros beetles. Because of their striking appearance, these beetles are collected by many people and are often displayed in museums and nature centers.

▼ A beetle is defeated.   A beetle is defeated in battle when it falls from the tree. The victor claims possession of the tree and its precious sap.

◄ **A male and female rhinoceros beetle meet.**

This female was attracted to the tree which was recently defended by the male rhinoceros beetle. Below the two rhinoceros beetles is a smaller stag beetle.

A male beetle defends his territory, a tree, for two reasons. First, it is his food source. But a tree is also a likely place to find a mate. In a large forest, it is difficult for males and females of the same species to find one another. But if the male has claimed a tree with good sap, he is likely to meet females because they will be attracted instinctively to the same kind of tree.

Not all beetles rely on this method of finding a mate. In many species, the female emits a strong odor, which attracts males of the same species to her.

► **A rhinoceros beetle and a stag beetle fighting.**

Stag beetles also gather at the same feeding area on the tree. Male stag beetles often lose if they fight with the larger, stronger rhinoceros beetles.

When a male rhinoceros beetle meets a female, he signals to her by bobbing his horns up and down. His abdomen also moves, and the front and hind wings touch each other, creating sounds. If the female does not ignore him, the male climbs on top of her and the two mate. The male's sperm are passed into the female's body. She stores them in special sacs in her abdomen until she is ready to lay her eggs. As the eggs pass out of her body, they are fertilized by the sperm.

◀ **Beetles mating (upper and lower photos).**

During the summer, male and female rhinoceros beetles meet and mate. When the male beetles have mated, they have fulfilled their purpose in life. When the tree sap stops flowing, in the fall, the males soon die.

▶ **A female rhinoceros beetle laying her eggs.**

After mating, the female flies around, looking for a place to lay her eggs. This beetle lays her eggs under the fallen leaves. The leaf mold makes a good hiding place and will provide food for the larvae.

▲ **Newly laid eggs.**

These newly laid eggs are about one-tenth of an inch long. They will soon double in size, and the shells will become hard and strong.

▲ **A larva emerging.**

In about ten days, the eggs are ready to hatch. Some beetle larvae have special "hatching spines" to help them. Others bite through the shell with their newly formed mandibles.

Some beetles lay only one egg at a time, other species lay up to 2,000 at once. Different species choose different places to lay their eggs. Some eggs are buried underground, some are attached to plant leaves and stems, others are placed in holes in trees. One type of scarab beetle, called the dung beetle, lays its eggs in animal manure. The eggs pictured here were laid beneath fallen leaves. The dead leaves make a warm hiding place for the eggs and will provide food for the rhinoceros beetle larvae when they emerge. Generally, the eggs are left to hatch on their own. So the female beetle is careful to place the eggs where the larvae will have plenty of food to eat.

▶ **A newly emerged larva.**

The newly emerged larvae are fragile and white. Gradually their bodies harden and take on color. Although these larvae do not have eyes, they are surrounded by food and have no trouble finding enough to eat.

◀ Beetle larvae emerging from the eggshell.

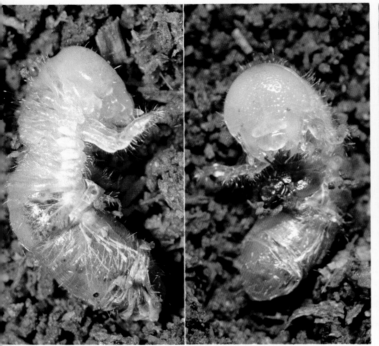

▲ **A beetle larva molting.**

The larvae of this species are not quite a half inch long when they first emerge. Within a week, they are an inch long and are ready to shed their skin for the first time.

▲ **A larva after molting.**

After molting, the larva's body is soft and transparent. The tube-like tracheae, visible through the skin, carry oxygen to every part of the larva's body. The brown spots are spiracles, holes for breathing.

The larva spends most of its time eating and growing. Because it eats almost constantly, it grows rapidly. But its hard skin does not grow with it, so the larva must molt, or shed its skin. Some beetles molt three times. Some molt as many as fourteen times before they are ready to enter the pupal stage of their life cycle.

When a larva is ready to molt, the old skin splits down the back. The larva's head appears first, then the rest of the body, as it wriggles out of the old skin. After it molts, the larva's body is soft and transparent. Gradually, the new skin hardens.

▶ **An oak forest in late autumn.**

▼ **A larva burrowing underground.**

The larva burrows underground, searching for food. The dug-up soil absorbs rain well, and the rain mixed with waste material from the larva provides nutritious soil for the trees in the forest.

▲ **Remnants of dead beetles.**   In the fall, when sap stops flowing in trees, most adult beetles die. Ants feast on these dead stag and rhinoceros beetles, leaving only the shell-like horns and thorax.

Beetles may spend the winter as eggs, larvae, or pupae, depending on the species and the climate. Few adult beetles live through the winter.

The larvae of this species of rhinoceros beetle burrow deep beneath the forest floor in winter, feeding on decaying leaves. The ground, covered with a thick blanket of fallen leaves, generates heat and helps keep the larvae warm. As the weather grows colder, the larvae burrow deeper and deeper.

But not all the larvae will live through the winter. Some will die of disease, and others will be eaten by moles or other underground animals. In spring, the larvae that have survived prepare to enter the next stage of their development, as they shape their pupal chambers. And so the life cycle of the beetle continues.

▶ **A larva makes a pupal chamber.**

In spring, the larvae that have survived the winter begin to shape their pupal chambers. Their bodies shrink, and their skin turns yellow. Within a week, they will become pupae.

▲ An oak grove in early summer.

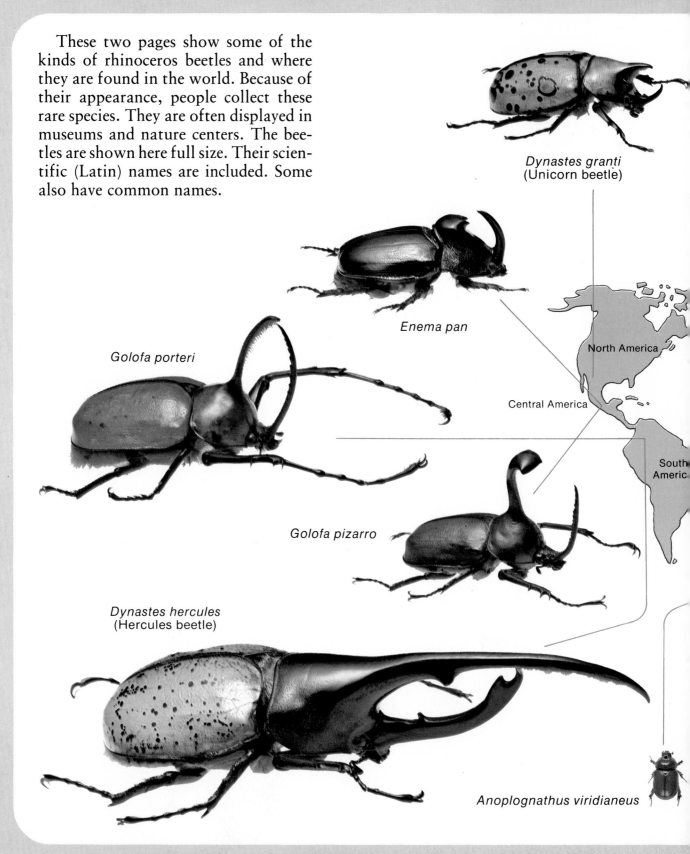

These two pages show some of the kinds of rhinoceros beetles and where they are found in the world. Because of their appearance, people collect these rare species. They are often displayed in museums and nature centers. The beetles are shown here full size. Their scientific (Latin) names are included. Some also have common names.

Dynastes granti
(Unicorn beetle)

Enema pan

Golofa porteri

North America

Central America

South America

Golofa pizarro

Dynastes hercules
(Hercules beetle)

Anoplognathus viridianeus

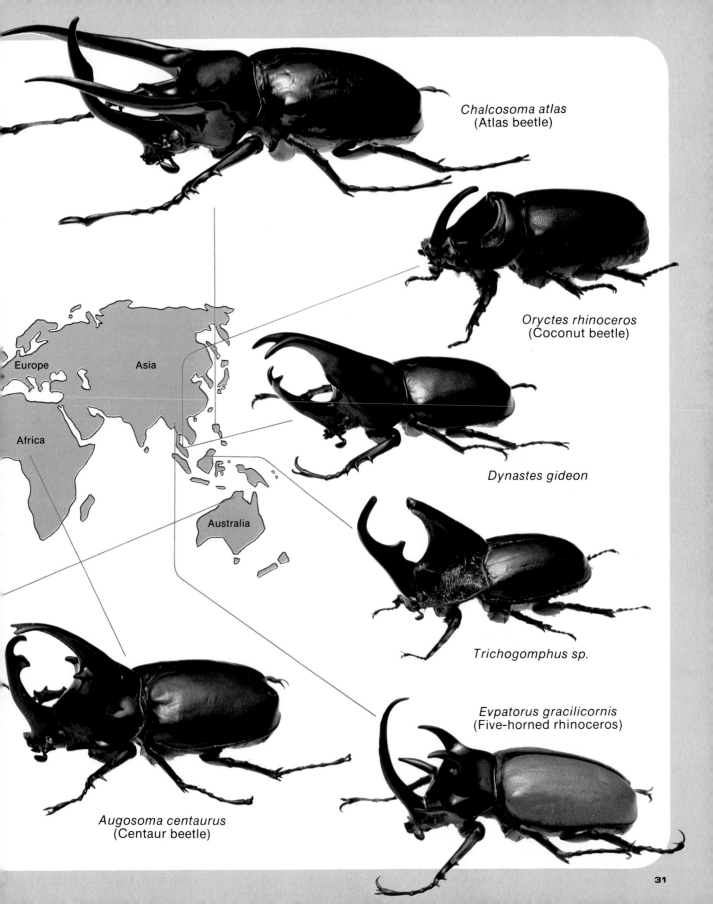

Chalcosoma atlas
(Atlas beetle)

Oryctes rhinoceros
(Coconut beetle)

Europe

Asia

Africa

Australia

Dynastes gideon

Trichogomphus sp.

Evpatorus gracilicornis
(Five-horned rhinoceros)

Augosoma centaurus
(Centaur beetle)

GLOSSARY

elytra—the beetle's front wings, which form a protective shell over the soft hind wings. (p. 16)

herbivorous—a word used to describe animals that eat plants. (p. 12)

instinct—behavior with which an animal is born, rather than behavior which is learned. (p. 20)

mandibles—jaws used for biting and chewing. (p. 12)

metamorphosis—a process of development during which physical changes take place. Complete metamorphosis involves four stages: egg, larva, pupa, and adult. Incomplete metamorphosis occurs in three stages: egg, nymph, and adult. (p. 7)

predators—animals that hunt or kill other animals for food. (p. 12)

proboscis—a tube-like mouth which is used for sucking liquids. (p. 14)

pupal chamber—a "room" which some species of beetles prepare for themselves as they are about to enter their pupal stage. (pp. 6, 7, 10)

scavengers—animals that feed on dead or decaying animal matter. (p. 12)

species—a group of animals which scientists have identified as having common traits. (pp. 4, 7, 12)